MW01148336

INVENTIONS
THAT CHANGED
THE WORLD

HENRY FORD

and the ASSEMBLY LINE

Angela Royston

PowerKiDS
press

NEW YORK

Published in 2016 by **The Rosen Publishing Group**
29 East 21st Street, New York, NY 10010

Produced for Rosen by Calcium

Editors for Calcium: Harriet McGregor and Sarah Eason
Designers: Jessica Moon and Paul Myerscough
Picture Research: Harriet McGregor

Picture credits: Cover: Getty Images: Interim Archives (fg), Print Collector (bkgd).
Insides: Dreamstime: Gunold Brunbauer 19, Marilyn Gould 5tr, Richard Gunion 26–27,
Johnny Habell 25, Jhernan124 12, Michal Nyvlt 22–23, Raytags 14, Rindradjaja 13, Sitikka
23, Thomas Vieth 21; Library of Congress: Detroit Publishing Co., 15; Shutterstock: Air
Images 11, Artens 27, Everett Collection 4–5, Filmfoto 10, Shu-Hung Liu 7, Olga Popova 6,
Raytags 28; Wikimedia Commons: 9, 17, Oregon Department of Transportation 18–19.

Cataloging-in-Publication Data
Royston, Angela.
Henry Ford and the assembly line / by Angela Royston.
p. cm. — (Inventions that changed the world)
Includes index.
ISBN 978-1-5081-4627-8 (pbk.)
ISBN 978-1-5081-4628-5 (6-pack)
ISBN 978-1-5081-4629-2 (library binding)
1. Ford, Henry, — 1863-1947 — Juvenile literature. 2. Automobile industry and trade
— United States — Biography — Juvenile literature. 3. Industrialists — United States —
Biography — Juvenile literature. I. Royston, Angela, 1945-. II. Title.
TL140.F6 R69 2016
338.7'6292—d23

Manufactured in the United States of America
CPSIA Compliance Information: Batch #BW16PK: For Further Information contact Rosen Publishing, New York, New York at 1-800-237-9932

CONTENTS

Changing the World 4

Who Was Henry Ford? 6

Gasoline Powers Early Cars 8

Finding the Money 10

The Model T 12

Large Numbers, Low Cost 14

Rolling Off the Assembly Line 16

Motor City 18

Controlling the Process 20

The United States at War 22

From Then to Now 24

Where Next? 26

Timeline 28

Glossary 30

For More Information 31

Index 32

CHANGING THE WORLD

Henry Ford changed the world by making cars available to millions of people and their families. He did not invent automobiles, but he figured out how to produce them cheaply, using a moving **assembly line**. His most successful car was the Model T, and between 1913 and 1927, it stormed the United States.

BEFORE HENRY

The world was a different place before Henry was born. Life was tough and travel was slow. Native Americans and European explorers walked, rode on horseback, and paddled canoes. Settlers moved west in covered wagons, drawn by teams of horses or oxen, in search of gold and new farmland. Travel speeded up after about 1860, when railroads were built and trains pulled by steam locomotives carried people and goods from coast to coast.

OIL CREEK

When oil was discovered at Oil Creek, Pennsylvania, in 1859, **engineers** realized it could be used to fuel engines to drive carriages, and the days of horse-drawn coaches were numbered. Less than 30 years later, the first automobile was invented. Henry was excited by these changes.

Before the invention of the automobile, people used horses and wagons to carry heavy goods.

Henry was not inclined to take no for an answer. He pursued his own ideals, despite setbacks. He later said:

"Whether you think you can or whether you think you can't, you are right."

He meant that expecting to succeed or fail is the most important part of success or failure.

BOOM TIME

By the 1920s, the Ford Motor Company was producing and selling two million new cars a year. Special factories were built to assemble automobiles and other vehicles. Workers came from the countryside and other countries to work in new US car plants, particularly those in Henry's home city of Detroit. Other industries sprang up to supply all kinds of goods, using Henry's successful methods. The world would never be the same again.

At first, cars were an expensive luxury and playthings for the very rich. Henry was determined to make them available to ordinary people.

WHO WAS HENRY FORD?

Henry Ford was born on July 30, 1863, in Greenfield Township not far from Detroit in Michigan. His parents were farmers and Henry was the eldest of six children. His father was eager for Henry to take over the farm, but Henry was more interested in machines and technology.

EXPERIMENTING AT HOME

Henry went to school until he was 15 years old, but he worked on the farm when he was not at school. At the same time he was fascinated by all kinds of machines. He found out about steam engines by talking to the men who worked on them, and he set up his own small machine store, where he used the most basic tools, such as screwdrivers and wire, to build a steam engine.

LEARNING BY WORKING

When Henry left school, he was determined to pursue engineering. He left the farm in 1879 and walked to Detroit, where he found work with a company that built railroad cars. This was followed by an **apprenticeship** in a machine store, making many kinds of machines. When he returned

Henry's early jobs taught him a lot about engineering and prepared him well for his work in the automobile trade. He was more than 40 years old by the time he was successful.

home in 1882, Henry put his knowledge to good use, improving the farm machinery and building a steam tractor. He married Clara Bryant in 1888, and his father, hoping that Henry would become a farmer, gave the couple their own farm.

RETURN TO DETROIT

Henry, however, was not about to give up his engineering ambitions. He moved to Detroit in 1891 to work as an engineer for the Edison Electric Illuminating Company, which generated electricity to power Edison's electric lamps. This gave Henry experience with electrical machines and time for his own inventions.

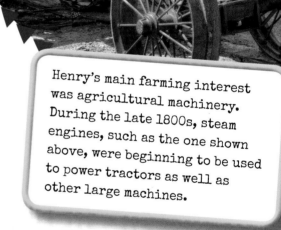

Henry's main farming interest was agricultural machinery. During the late 1800s, steam engines, such as the one shown above, were beginning to be used to power tractors as well as other large machines.

Like Clockwork

When Henry was 15 years old, his father gave him a pocket watch. This was a small clock on a chain that men attached to their waistcoats. Henry, however, dismantled his watch to learn how it worked. He learned so well that he was able to repair other people's watches when they broke!

GASOLINE POWERS EARLY CARS

Henry's experience with steam tractors made him realize that steam engines could power tractors and locomotives, but were too cumbersome to produce a fast and reliable self-propelled carriage. Scientists had already invented engines that ran on gasoline and in 1886, in Germany, Karl Benz produced the first automobile fueled by gasoline. Henry wanted to do the same.

REVOLUTIONARY ENGINE

An **internal combustion engine** produces power by burning fuel inside the engine. In 1876, Nikolaus Otto, a German engineer, built the first engine to successfully burn gasoline. It used a **piston** inside a cylinder. As fuel exploded inside the cylinder, it pushed the piston down. The piston was connected to a **crankshaft**, which turned as the piston moved up and down.

FIRST PRACTICAL AUTOMOBILE

Karl Benz made history in 1886, when he produced the first gas-powered automobile. The vehicle was nicknamed a "horseless carriage" because it looked like a carriage but was propelled by an engine, not horses.

HENRY'S QUADRICYCLE

Although Henry was working for Edison during the day, he was thinking about the work of Otto and Benz the rest of the time. In 1892, with the help of his wife Clara, he built a small gasoline engine in his kitchen sink. He went on to develop a better engine and used it to power the Quadricycle, which he built in his woodshed. In 1896, Henry was the only person in Detroit to own a car, and he drove it for 1,000 miles (1,600 km) before he sold it to raise money to develop his next automobile.

Henry and his wife, Clara, enjoyed driving the Quadricycle through the streets of Henry's home city, Detroit, Michigan.

Brayton's Ready Motor

Henry was not the first American to build a gasoline-powered carriage. In 1872, George Brayton **patented** a different type of internal combustion engine than Otto's. The engine, however, used to **backfire** and explode. George Seldon used a similar, smaller engine in his Seldon Auto in 1895. He produced one working model, but later claimed, unsuccessfully, that Henry had stolen his ideas.

FINDING THE MONEY

Henry did not have enough money to develop his next car and had to find business people who would back him. The Edison Electric Illuminating Company was not interested in gasoline cars, so Henry left the company to strike out on his own.

GETTING GOING

Henry's first company went bankrupt as a result of his lack of business experience. His second company, the Henry Ford Company, was more successful until Henry fell out with his backers, who wanted to produce expensive cars for wealthy people. Henry, however, was determined to produce a car for ordinary people and in 1902, he left the company, which later became Cadillac.

This car was built in 1903, but still works today, taking part in "old-timer" rallies. Like Henry's Quadricycle, it is steered using a rudder, not a steering wheel.

RACING TO VICTORY

For the next year, Henry concentrated on racing cars. He built two cars, the "999" and the "Arrow," to show that cars could be fast and reliable. Barney Oldfield, a famous driver, won every race he entered in the "Arrow," but Henry's greatest success was when "999" won at Grosse Pointe in October 1902. The prize money and the publicity brought the backing Henry needed, and in 1903, he set up the Ford Motor Company. One year later the company moved production to a new building on Piquette Avenue, Detroit.

Henry paved the way for car ownership to become commonplace for modern-day families.

IDENTICAL PARTS

At the same time, Henry looked for ways to reduce the price of his cars. Every part of an early car was made by hand and adjusted to fit. Henry knew that some industries, such as gun manufacturers, used identical, standard parts to make production faster and easier.

The Word Is...

Henry spelled out his vision for an affordable family car:

"I will build a motor car for the great multitude . . . constructed of the best materials, by the best men to be hired, after the simplest designs that modern engineering can devise . . . so low in price that no man making a good salary will be unable to own one . . . ."

THE MODEL T

Once Henry had set up the Ford Motor Company in 1903, he employed a team of skillful engineers and together they worked on the design of a simple, basic car. They took ideas and inventions from other companies and adapted them to improve their own designs. Their first car, the Model A, was followed by the Model N, before finally, in 1908, they produced the Model T.

THE TIN LIZZIE

The Model T was often known as the Tin Lizzie, probably because it was basically an engine inside a metal box on wheels. It was not made of tin, however, but of vanadium steel, a special, lightweight steel made in France. Henry came across vanadium steel by accident, in the wreckage of a French racing car, and he realized it was the ideal material for his cars.

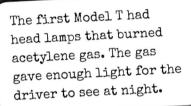

The first Model T had head lamps that burned acetylene gas. The gas gave enough light for the driver to see at night.

THE ENGINE

The Model T was powered by an internal combustion engine with four cylinders. The piston in each cylinder turned the wheels only one-quarter of the time, making the power jerky. Two cylinders were better, but it took four cylinders to give continuous power. The spark to light the fuel was provided by a device called a **magneto**, which used a spinning **flywheel** to generate electricity and was much simpler than the batteries used by most other cars at that time.

Instant Success

More than 10,000 Model T Fords were sold in 1908, the first year the car was produced. The sale price of $825 was reduced as sales increased. By 1914, the car sold for $575. Henry could easily sell every car he produced, but he said he wanted to produce as many cars as he could sell.

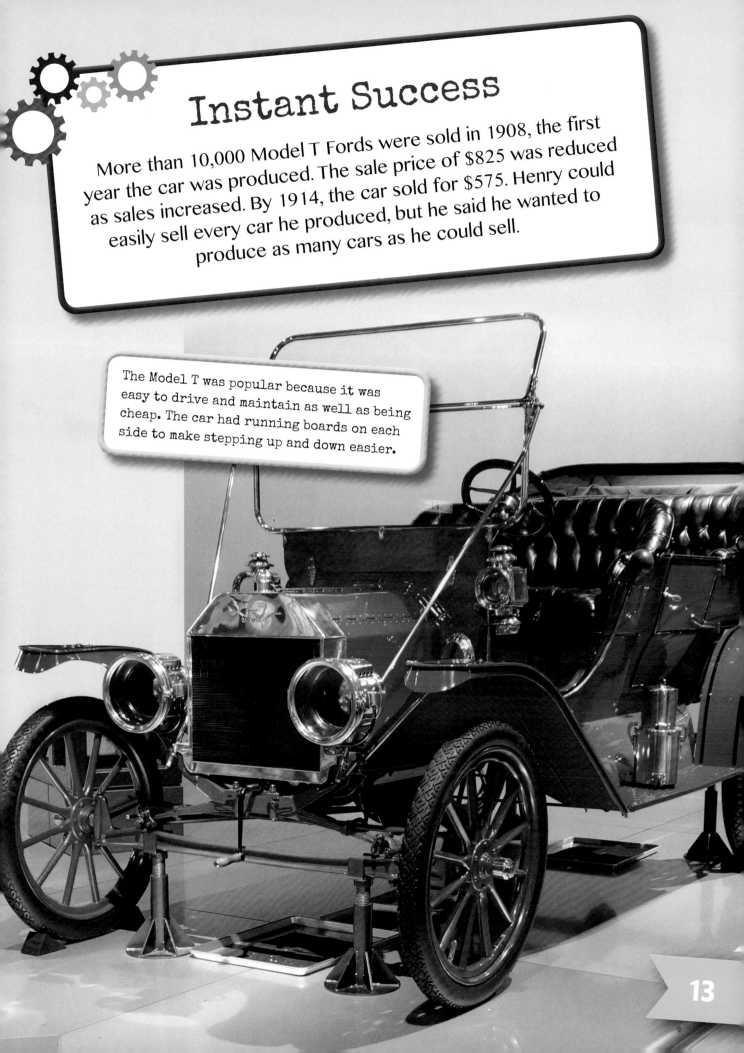

The Model T was popular because it was easy to drive and maintain as well as being cheap. The car had running boards on each side to make stepping up and down easier.

LARGE NUMBERS, LOW COST

Early cars were constructed by a team of workers who made and assembled all the parts of the car. It was skilled but slow work, and only a few cars were completed each day. Henry sped up the process by assembling the parts separately and introducing an assembly line. In this way he produced many more cars far more cheaply.

OLDSMOBILES LEAD THE WAY

An assembly line begins with the basic frame of the car to which the other parts, such as the wheels, the engines, and the seats, are added little by little. Henry was not the first person to use an assembly line to build cars. In 1901, Ransom Olds introduced standardized parts and an assembly line to produce his

Oldsmobile pioneered the use of identical parts and an assembly line to produce cars, including this stylish, shiny "horseless carriage" made in 1904.

Curved Dash Oldsmobiles. By using identical **valves**, screws, and the same basic pieces, a team of workers could quickly assemble identical components. Production increased to 20 cars per day.

SPEEDING UP THE LINE

In the first assembly lines the car stayed still and the workers moved along the line, adding their part to the car. Henry realized that the process would be faster if the workers stayed in one place and the assembly line moved from one group to the next. He got the idea after visiting a meat-packer in Chicago. There, whole carcasses of beef hung from a moving trolley and each meat-packer sliced off and packaged a particular cut of meat.

HIGHLAND PARK PLANT

In 1910, Henry moved the production of the Model T from Piquette Avenue to a new, larger site in Highland Park, Detroit. This building was specially designed to produce multiple, identical copies of the Ford Model T.

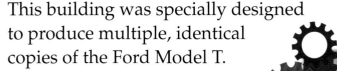

The Word Is...

Standardized parts meant that customers had less choice. In 1909, Henry announced:

"Any customer can have a car painted any color that he wants so long as it is black!"

When Henry opened his historic Highland Plant at 91 Manchester Avenue in Highland Park, Michigan (shown here), it began a revolution in mass production.

ROLLING OFF THE ASSEMBLY LINE

Henry copied the Chicago meat-packer's assembly line, but turned it back to front. His assembly line produced a finished car from its component parts. Henry figured out all the actions needed to produce each component and all the actions needed to assemble it. Then he trained his workers to specialize in just one action.

MOVING IT ALONG

Henry introduced his moving assembly line in 1913. At first the basic frame was hauled by ropes along a line of workers, who added a specific piece or carried out a specific action as the car passed. Then Henry introduced a moving conveyor belt, which sped up the process considerably.

ASSEMBLING THE PARTS

The main parts of the cars, including the engine, the magneto, the brakes, and the dash, were assembled separately. Each part consisted of standardized components, so once the system was set, the workers simply had to do the same thing time after time.

REPETITIVE STRAIN

Assembly lines changed a skilled job into a simple, repetitive action, at a pace driven by the conveyor belt. This was stressful, boring work, and most workers stayed only a few months. To stop his workers from leaving, Henry doubled their pay. They were then so well paid, they put up with the boredom. Henry also reduced the hours they worked so that he could fit in two shifts and keep the factory working day and night!

Go Figure!

To measure the time taken to produce something you must take into account the number of people involved. For example, a man-hour is the equivalent of one man working for one hour. In 1903, it took 12.5 man-hours to assemble a basic car in one spot. The rope-pulled assembly line reduced the time to 6 man-hours. By 1914, the time had been cut to an incredible 93 man-minutes.

MOTOR CITY

Model Ts were so successful that by the early 1920s, they accounted for more than half of all cars produced in the United States, and they were so cheap Henry's car workers could buy them with just two months' salary. The combination of **mass production**, low prices, and high wages became known as "Fordism." As other companies copied Henry's methods, Detroit became the center of a powerful and flourishing motor industry.

MOTOWN

By the 1920s, the three biggest automakers were Ford, General Motors, and Chrysler, and all were based in Detroit. Other famous automakers in Detroit included Oldsmobile, Dodge, Buick, and Cadillac. Workers flocked to Detroit to get jobs in the automobile plants. They came from the countryside around Detroit and from across the United States. They also came from other countries, in particular Mexico and countries throughout Europe.

BRINGING CHANGE

The success of the auto industry fueled an economic boom in the United States, which lasted through the 1920s. Companies started up to produce specialized parts, such as tires. Steel mills expanded to supply steel for car bodywork. Other specialist companies supplied glass for the windshields, or leather for the seats, or one of the other materials needed to build cars. Thousands of miles of new roads with tarred surfaces were built within and between cities.

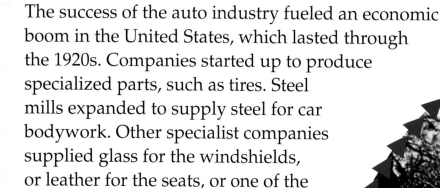

Constructing roads to carry new automobiles created thousands of jobs for Americans.

In 1920, wealthy people enjoyed driving a Mercedes Benz sports car on the open road. Today's vintage car collectors love the same car.

Best Buy

It was not just the price that made the Model T so popular. With only two forward **gears** and a reverse pedal, it was easier to drive than other cars. The engine was so basic it was simple to repair if it broke down. In the 1920s, most roads in the United States were rutted, bumpy dirt roads. Unlike the heavy, rigid frame of other cars, the Model T's frame was lightweight and flexible so it could ride the bumps more easily. It could even be driven over fields and through shallow rivers.

CONTROLLING THE PROCESS

As the United States boomed and workers became richer, sales of the Model T began to fall. There were more makes and models of car for people to choose from and many of them were more stylish than the Model T. Henry decided to cut costs by owning his own suppliers. At the same time his son, Edsel, who now officially ran the company, argued that they needed to produce a new, more up-to-date model.

THE ROUGE COMPLEX

In 1915, Henry acquired a huge site on the Rouge River in Dearborn, near Detroit, where he planned to produce everything from raw materials to finished vehicles. He built steel furnaces, glass furnaces, and **rolling mills**. He also bought coal mines, forests, and iron mines in states such as Michigan, Minnesota, and Pennsylvania. He acquired steamships and built his own railroad to transport materials directly to the Rouge Complex. In 1921, the Fordson, the world's first mass-produced tractor, was made at the Rouge.

THE LAST MODEL T

Components for the Model T were produced at the Rouge but sent to Highland Park to be assembled. Edsel, however, knew that the Model T was beginning to fail, and tried to persuade his father to produce a new, more expensive auto. Henry did not want to change something that had been so successful. Eventually, he could no longer ignore the sales figures and accepted that the Model T's days were over. In 1927, as the 15 millionth Model T became the last one to roll off the Highland Park Plant, the more stylish Model A went into production at the Rouge.

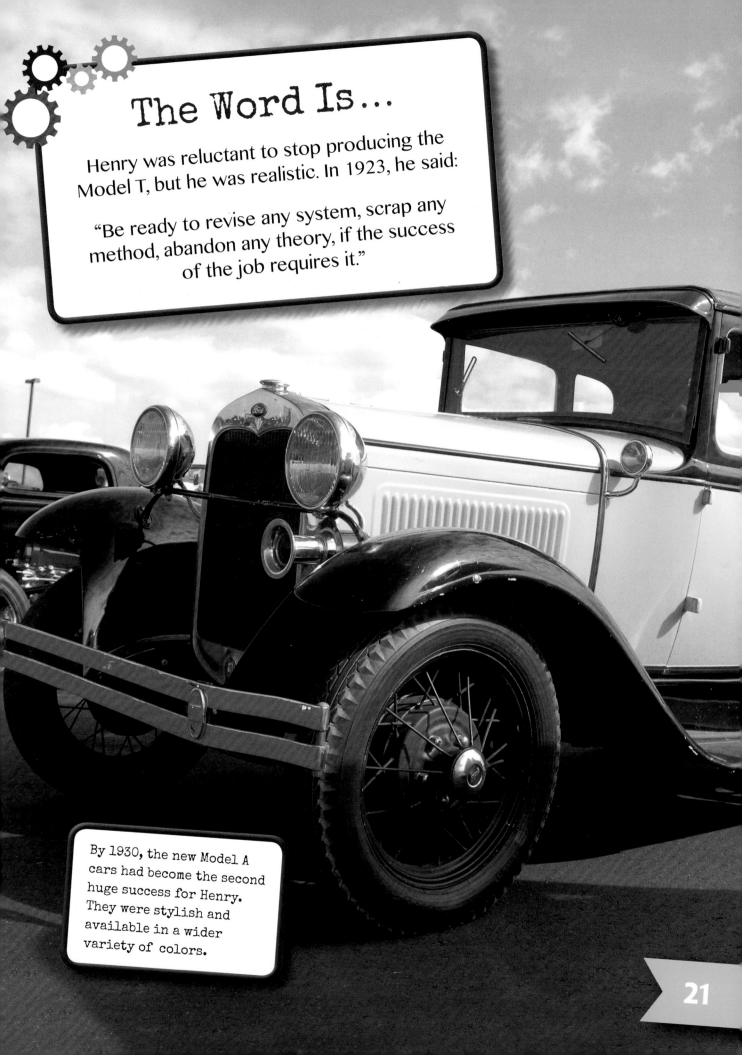

The Word Is...

Henry was reluctant to stop producing the Model T, but he was realistic. In 1923, he said:

"Be ready to revise any system, scrap any method, abandon any theory, if the success of the job requires it."

By 1930, the new Model A cars had become the second huge success for Henry. They were stylish and available in a wider variety of colors.

THE UNITED STATES AT WAR

By the 1930s, more than 100,000 people worked at the Rouge. The site included 93 buildings, making various vehicles from raw materials to finished cars. When the United States entered World War II (1939–1945) in December, 1941, the Rouge and all of Detroit's other automobile companies stopped making cars and started making jeeps, tanks, and fighter and bomber aircraft engines.

LIBERATOR BOMBERS

In January, 1940, the Roosevelt government persuaded the Ford Company to produce much needed bomber aircraft. On March 28, 1941, work began to clear a forest at Ypsilanti, about 30 miles (50 km) west of Detroit. This became the site of the Willow Run plant, where all of Henry's technical know-how was used to organize and build production and assembly lines for B24 Liberator bombers. The plant employed 42,000 workers and by early 1945 had produced 8,600 B24 bombers.

Henry was a pacifist, which means that he did not support war. He hated "our boys" being killed, but he agreed to produce vehicles to protect them.

HANDING OVER

In 1919, Henry appointed his son Edsel as president of the company, although Henry remained actively involved. Sadly, Edsel died in 1943, and Henry took over as president again. By 1945, Henry was 80 years old and he again handed over the company, this time to his grandson Henry Ford II. Henry himself died on April 7, 1947, at his home in Dearborn.

Ambulances produced for the army in Detroit were shipped across the Atlantic Ocean. They were used in the allied armies' advance through Europe.

Right-Hand Man

Charles Sorensen worked closely with Henry for 40 years, from 1905 through 1945. He helped design the assembly line for the Model T and, later, the Fordson tractor. At the Rouge he became one of Henry's "right-hand men," and in 1940, he designed the assembly line at Willow Run in just one night. He wrote: "As I look back now upon that night, this was the biggest challenge of my production career." He promised the government that the plant would produce a B24 every hour. He kept his promise!

FROM THEN TO NOW

After World War II, automobiles became bigger and better. From 1945 through 1970, motor manufacturers made more money than ever before or since. Multilane highways were built to take all the vehicles using the roads. Since 1970, robots have taken over on the production lines, and US motor manufacturers have faced increasing competition from companies in Europe and the Far East.

GAS GUZZLERS

In the 1950s and 1960s, automobiles became larger and more streamlined with faster, bigger engines. Gas was cheap and the new cars consumed gallons of it. Automobiles were the main method of transport and often became the center of social life, with drive-in movies, drive-in banks, and even drive-in church services.

COMPETITION FROM ABROAD

As motor manufacturers in Japan, Korea, other Far Eastern countries, and Europe exported more cars, fewer cars on US roads were made in the United States. Automobiles became more efficient as a result of better engineering and computers.

ROBOTS

Robots are machines that are controlled by computers. They were first used in car manufacturing to **weld** and to paint. In 1961, General Motors became the first company to add a robotic arm to the assembly line. Today, the whole assembly line is operated by robots, which are programmed to add each piece of car at exactly the right time. Robots are more reliable and faster than people and they do not demand wages! Even drivers may soon be replaced by computers. Cars are already being designed that are controlled and operated by computers.

More and More Cars

This table shows the dramatic rise in the number of cars produced in China and Korea in 2014 compared with 2000.

Country	Number of cars produced in:	
	2014	2000
China	19,919,795	604,677
Japan	8,277,070	8,359,434
Germany	5,604,026	5,131,918
United States	4,253,098	5,542,217
South Korea	4,124,116	2,602,008

Traffic fills freeways in Los Angeles and in other large cities around the world. Exhaust fumes produced by the vehicles pollute the air, while freeways and parking spaces take up large areas of city land.

WHERE NEXT?

Henry's legacy was a boom in mass-produced goods, particularly cars, which brought jobs and a better standard of living to workers in many countries, including the United States. Today, however, the world is facing new challenges, and these are partly due to Henry's tremendous success. Many towns and cities across the world are congested with traffic and polluted by fumes. The fumes are contributing to an even greater threat, climate change.

TROUBLESOME GASES

When vehicles burn gas, they produce carbon dioxide and other gases as waste fumes, which disperse into the air. They add to millions of tons of carbon dioxide produced by burning oil, coal, and gas for other purposes. Carbon dioxide in the air acts like a hothouse, trapping heat from the sun and warming the atmosphere. Warmer temperatures are changing climates and producing extreme weather that threatens millions of lives.

Like this Toyota, the cleanest cars are powered by hydrogen fuel cells. The cell uses hydrogen to produce electricity for the electric motor. The only exhaust is water vapor and no carbon dioxide is released.

CLEANER CARS

Engineers in the motor industry have been figuring out how to produce cleaner, carbon-free technology. Automobiles now have more efficient engines that use less gas. Some cars run on electricity or have two engines, an electric one and a small gasoline one. The problem is that the cleanest cars are expensive to buy. Today, we need a new Henry Ford to make cars that do not burn oil, gas, or coal but are cheap enough for most people to buy!

Small electric cars are becoming more popular. Many cities have special parking points where the batteries of the cars can be recharged.

The Word Is...

Even before climate change was a problem, Henry was aware that the motor industry damaged the environment and used up valuable resources.
In 1935, he wrote:

"I foresee the time when industry shall no longer denude the forests which require generations to mature, nor use up the mines, which were ages in making, but shall draw its raw material largely from the annual produce of the fields."

TIMELINE

1859 Oil is discovered at Oil Creek, Pennsylvania.

1863 Henry Ford is born on July 30, in Greenfield Township, Michigan.

1872 George Brayton becomes the first American to patent an internal combustion engine.

1876 Nikolaus Otto builds the first successful gasoline engine.

1879 Henry moves to Detroit and works in various engineering jobs.

1882 Henry returns to his father's farm where he works on farm machinery and builds a steam tractor.

The Model T, the first affordable car, gave the driver a bumpy ride at speeds of up to 45 miles (72 km) per hour.

1886 Karl Benz builds the first successful self-propelled automobile fueled by gasoline.

1888 Henry marries Clara Bryant.

1891 Henry moves to Detroit to work as an engineer for the Edison Electric Illuminating Company.

1892 Henry and Clara build a small gasoline engine in their kitchen sink.

1893 Henry's son, Edsel Bryant, is born on November 6.

1895 George Seldon builds a working model of a gasoline-powered automobile.

1896 Henry builds the Quadricycle.

1899 Henry forms his first company, the Detroit Automobile Company, which goes bankrupt in 1900.

1901 Henry builds successful racing cars. He forms his second company, the Henry Ford Company. Ransom Olds uses standardized parts and an assembly line to produce the Oldsmobile Curved Dash.

1902 Henry leaves his second company in March after an argument. Barney Oldfield wins the Manufacturer's Cup Challenge at Grosse Pointe driving Henry's racing car "999."

1903 Henry sets up his third company, the Ford Motor Company.

1904 Builds and moves into a new plant on Piquette Avenue, Detroit.

1907 Work begins on designing the Model T.

1908 The first Model T is produced at the Piquette plant.

1910 Production moves from Piquette Plant to Highland Park Plant.

1913 Henry introduces his moving assembly line.

1914 Henry increases workers' pay and reduces their hours.

1915 Buys a large area of land at Dearborn alongside the Rouge River.

1917 Begins building a huge plant that includes almost every aspect of manufacturing an automobile from iron ore to finished car.

1919 Henry's son, Edsel, is appointed President of the Ford Motor Company.

1921 The world's first mass-produced tractor, the Fordson, is produced at the Rouge Complex.

1920s Many roads are improved or built, including the New York parkway system.

1927 Chevrolet takes over the top spot for car sales. The 15 millionth and final Model T car leaves the assembly line at Highland Park Plant.

1927 The new Model A Ford goes into production at the Rouge Plant.

1940 Motor manufacturers in Detroit stop producing cars and change to military vehicles and engines.

1941 Work begins on clearing land at Ypsilanti for the Willow Run Plant. On December 11, the United States enters World War II following the Japanese attack on the US naval fleet in Pearl Harbor in Hawaii.

1943 Henry's son Edsel dies. Henry takes over as President of the company.

1945 World War II ends. Ford Motor Company returns to automobile and truck production.

1947 Henry Ford dies on April 7.

1956 The federal government passes an act authorizing the building of the Interstate Highway system.

1961 General Motors introduces a robotic arm into the assembly line.

1980s Robots increasingly used on car assembly lines worldwide.

1986 The I-80 becomes the first freeway to connect the Atlantic coast to the Pacific coast. It joins New York City to San Francisco.

2012 First US license for a self-driven car is issued in Nevada.

apprenticeship Learning a skill by working with an expert.

assembly line A system for putting together the parts that make up a machine or object by adding the parts one by one as the machine or object is moved along a line.

backfire An improperly timed explosion of fuel mixture in the cylinder of an internal combustion engine.

crankshaft A rod that changes the upward and downward movement of a piston into a turning movement. In a car, the crankshaft is connected to other rods, which turn the wheels.

engineers People who use science to design or make machines or construct large objects such as bridges.

flywheel A heavy, spinning wheel that stores energy. A magneto uses the movement to generate electricity.

gears Devices that change the speed of an engine.

internal combustion engine An engine that produces power by burning fuel to move a piston inside a cylinder.

magneto A small electric generator used by internal combustion engines to produce electric sparks to burn fuel.

mass production Method of manufacturing a large number of identical items at low cost using machines.

patented Given a license that stops anyone else from making, using, or selling the same invention.

piston A solid cylinder that fits inside a hollow cylinder and moves back and forth as gases in the cylinder expand and contract.

rolling mills Buildings where metal is made into bars and flat plates or sheets.

valves Devices that allow a gas or liquid to flow only in a particular direction.

weld To use heat to join two pieces of metal by melting them together.

Books

Burgan, Michael. *Who Was Henry Ford?* New York, NY: Grosset & Dunlap, 2014.

El Nabli, Dina. *Henry Ford* (TIME for Kids: Biographies). New York, NY: HarperCollins Children's Books, 2008.

Gregory, Josh. *Henry Ford: Father of the Auto Industry* (A True Book). New York, NY: Scholastic, 2013.

Harris, Nicholas. *How It Works: Car.* Hauppauge, NY: Barron's Educational Series, 2010.

Reis, Ronald A. *Henry Ford* (For Kids). Chicago, IL: Chicago Review Press, 2016.

Sich, Jenny. *100 Inventions That Made History*. New York, NY: DK Publishing, 2014.

Websites

Due to the changing nature of Internet links, PowerKids Press has developed an online list of websites related to the subject of this book. This site is updated regularly. Please use this link to access the list: **www.powerkidslinks.com/itctw/ford**

INDEX

A

assembly line, 4, 14–17, 22–24, 28–29

B

Benz, Karl, 8, 28
Brayton, George, 9, 28

C

climate change, 26–27

E

engineers, 4, 7–8, 12, 27–28
engines, 4, 6, 8–9, 12, 14, 16, 19, 22, 24, 27–29

F

Ford, Edsel, 20, 23, 28–29
Ford II, Henry, 23
Ford Motor Company, 5, 11–12, 28–29

G

gasoline, 8–10, 27–28
General Motors, 18, 24, 29

H

Highland Park Plant, 15, 20, 29

I

internal combustion engine, 8–9, 12, 28

M

Model A, 12, 20, 29
Model T, 4, 12–13, 15, 18–21, 23, 29

O

oil, 4, 26–28
Oldfield, Barney, 11, 28
Olds, Ransom, 14, 28
Oldsmobiles, 14–15, 18, 28
Otto, Nikolaus, 8–9, 28

Q

Quadricycle, 8, 28

R

railroads, 4, 6, 20
roads, 18–19, 24, 29
robots, 24, 29
Rouge Complex, 20, 22–23, 29

S

Seldon, George, 9, 28
Sorensen, Charles, 23

T

trains, 4

W

war, 22–24, 29
workers, 5, 14–18, 20, 22, 26, 29